Forew
Nancy DeMo

LIVING OUT THE *One Anothers* OF SCRIPTURE

A 30-Day Devotional

Revive Our Hearts™

Living Out the One Anothers of Scripture

Published by *Revive Our Hearts*
P.O. Box 2000
Niles, MI 49120

© 2020 Revive Our Hearts

Hayley Mullins, Managing Editor
Erin Davis, Content Manager

Printed in the United States of America

ISBN: 978-1-934718-75-9

Scripture quotations, unless otherwise indicated, are from the ESV® Bible (The Holy Bible, English Standard Version®), copyright © 2001 by Crossway, a publishing ministry of Good News Publishers. Used by permission. All rights reserved.

Scripture quotations marked CSB have been taken from the Christian Standard Bible®, Copyright © 2017 by Holman Bible Publishers. Used by permission. Christian Standard Bible® and CSB® are federally registered trademarks of Holman Bible Publishers.

Scriptures marked KJV are taken from the King James Version.

Emphasis in Scripture quotations added by the authors.

TABLE OF CONTENTS

Part I: *Your Attitude*

Part II: *Your Presence*

Foreword

A number of years ago, I found myself sitting on a set of hard bleachers, cheering for some of my friends' kids who were playing in a junior high basketball game. Our team was trailing badly. The poor boys grew increasingly exhausted and discouraged. But instead of encouraging one another, they began to pick on each other.

Those of us who were seated in the stands watched helplessly as these kids began to compete against each other instead of against the other team! As a result they became even more frustrated, downhearted, and ineffective. I can't recall the final outcome of that game, but I know what we witnessed that day looks a lot like our lives and relationships at times—even in the Body of Christ.

As followers of Jesus, we are on the same team, a team owned, selected, and coached by God Himself. Through His Word, God gives clear guidance on how we can build up our fellow teammates.

"Comfort one another." (2 Cor. 13:11)
"Build one another up." (1 Thess. 5:11)
"Serve one another." (Gal. 5:13)

And unlike what I witnessed at the ball game that day, we are supposed to encourage one another (Heb. 10:25).

There are lots more "one anothers" in Scripture. "Do not speak evil against one another" (James 4:11). "Do not grumble against one another" (James 5:9). "Confess your sins to one another and pray for one another, that you may be healed" (James 5:16).

What a joy it is to belong to God's team and to know that we don't have to live the Christian life by ourselves.

None of us can become spiritually mature or have a fruitful life if we're not consistently on both the giving and receiving end of these "one anothers" found in God's Word. We all need to be encouraged, exhorted, rebuked, forgiven, prayed for, and built up by those who heed God's command to "love one another" (John 13:34).

How grateful I am for the people in my life who help me become more like Jesus by practicing these and other "one anothers." I want to fulfill my responsibility to demonstrate Christ's love to them in return.

The resource you are holding in your hands has been developed by some of our *Revive Our Hearts* writers to help you discover and live out the "one anothers" of Scripture.

As you walk through this thirty-day devotional, ask the Lord to show you how you can build up the believers around you with these important, life-giving "one anothers." May God's Word remind you of the responsibility and privilege it is to be on His team, and may His Spirit enable you to faithfully care for the "one anothers" in your life.

Nancy DeMoss Wolgemuth

Introduction

Start to look for them in your Bible, and you will find them everywhere—the "one anothers." They are a series of commands for how the image-bearers of God (that's us!) are to treat our fellow image-bearers.

We find one here . . .

"Outdo one another in showing honor" (Rom. 12:10).

Another one here . . .

"Comfort one another" (2 Cor. 13:11).

And still another one right here . . .

"Confess your sins to one another and pray for one another" (James 5:16).

Pile all of the "one anothers" into one big, beautiful box, and you could wrap it neatly with this bow: "For this is the message that you have heard from the beginning, that we should love one another" (1 John 3:11).

Love one another.

Perhaps it feels like an overly simplistic solution to a world so broken by sin. Or maybe, more likely, you've tried it, and found the "others" in the "one anothers" difficult to love. And yet over and over throughout His Word, God repeats this command.

"Love one another" (John 13:34).

"Love one another" (John 15:12).

"Love one another" (Rom. 12:10).

All of the other "one anothers" flow from this single expectation.

That beautiful box filled with the bow I mentioned to you before? It is indeed a gift. These are treasured principles for how to live with each other in harmony. And where there is a gift, there is always a gift-giver. In this case, the Giver is Jesus, the God of love. He modeled the statements you'll read about in this devotional by loving us first (and loving us still).

When the rules for engagement with the others around us war against our flesh, we look toward Another who is not one of us. We ask Him to transform our hearts to become more like His so we can treat others the way His Word commands us to.

For the next thirty days, enjoy spending time with the "one anothers" of Scripture. As you do, may you be encouraged to love the "one anothers" all around you.

PART I:
Your Attitude

Adopt the same attitude
as that of Christ Jesus,
who . . . emptied himself
by assuming the form of a servant.

PHILIPPIANS 2:5–7 CSB

DAY 1

Therefore let us not pass judgment on one another any longer, but rather decide never to put a stumbling block or hindrance in the way of a brother.

ROMANS 14:13

LET US NOT PASS JUDGMENT
ON *One Another*

Perhaps it was a cucumber. I suppose it could have been a carrot, a turnip, or a bunch of kale. Scripture doesn't tell us what it was exactly, but Romans 14 does reveal that the people of God were looking down their noses at each other. What was the source of scorn, exactly? Vegetables. Yep, vegetables.

"One person believes he may eat anything," the apostle Paul wrote, "while the weak person eats only vegetables. Let not the one who eats despise the one who abstains, and let not the one who abstains pass judgment on the one who eats" (vv. 2–3).

There are passages in Scripture that warn us against judging another person's *sins* unless we want the same measuring stick applied to our sin (Matt. 7:1–5). This is a different kind of warning. Paul is warning us not to judge other Christian's *preferences.*

- Perhaps you homeschool and another mom in your church sends her children to public school. That's a preference.
- Maybe your family watches PG-13 movies and your sister's family doesn't own a television. Preference.
- You love one Bible translation and your Bible study leader likes another.
- Your kids never miss church for sports; your friend's kids see sports as their mission field.
- You love upbeat worship music; your husband likes the old hymns.
- Preference. Preference. Preference.

When we feel judgment toward another believer, when we dislike their choices or convince ourselves they are somehow less spiritual than us because of them, isn't a preference usually to blame? How many churches and friendships have split over preference disguised as principle?

In contrast, God's Word urges us to extend grace, not judgment, toward one another.

"Therefore let us not pass judgment on one another any longer, but rather decide never to put a stumbling block or hindrance in the way of a brother" (Rom. 14:13).

Grace is a decision. A choice you can make when a Christian brother or sister has a preference that is different from yours. Paul reminds us why: "for God has welcomed him" (v. 3).

Since the "one anothers" in your world are welcomed by Christ, you are free to welcome them, too. Welcome them into your heart. Welcome them into your church. Welcome them into your home, free of judgment.

Who knows? They might even bring you some vegetables.

CONSIDER:

How does the gospel impact the everyday ways we respond to other Christians? Since we are accepted by Christ through His grace, not our perfection, how does this color the way we view the choices of others who are in Him?

_____

_____

_____

_____

_____

_____

PRAY:

Ask God to reveal any evidence of a critical spirit toward other believers. Repent for any exposed judgment toward your Christian brothers and sisters.

TRUST:

If something needs adjusted in the life of a fellow believer, or in your own, you can trust God to do it through the power of the Holy Spirit.

> "Nevertheless, I tell you the truth: it is to your advantage that I go away, for if I do not go away, the Helper will not come to you. But if I go, I will send him to you. And when he comes, he will convict the world concerning sin and righteousness and judgment." (John 16:7-8)

DO:

Choose to celebrate your Christian brothers and sisters who chose differently than you. Shoot a text to a Christian friend who has a different preference than you and tell her how much you admire her.

DAY 2

Let us not become conceited . . .
enving one another.

GALATIANS 5:26

LET US NOT ENVY
One Another

The Filipinos have a phrase, *isip talangka*. You might have heard it said this way: crab mentality.

The best way to explain this idea is to picture a bunch of crabs, all caught by an intrepid fisherman and thrown together in a bucket. If one of them tries to escape, the others will all pull him back down. Escape is impossible because each crab won't let anyone get ahead of them. In the end, they *all* get eaten.

"If I can't have it, neither can you"—a perfect picture of *envy*.

Envy says, "I'm more important. And I deserve this. You *definitely* don't. I'd rather we all fail than you succeed."

You may know the tenth commandment, "You shall not covet your neighbor's wife, or his male servant, or his female servant, or his ox, or his donkey, or anything that is your neighbor's" (Ex. 20:17). In other words, don't get your heart set on what others have.

Relationships, status, wealth, personality, achievements . . . they all can become the object of our coveting. But what happens when we not only *want* what our neighbor has, we decide that we don't like the fact that our neighbor has it at all? That, my friends, is envy.

Envy fixates on another person. It's not only wishing that you had what they have but also wishing that *they didn't* have it. It's coveting that's teamed up with resentment. It's a knife of desire, sharpened to an edge of hatred.

Truly envy is deadly—to our own souls and to the lives of others.

Think about it. Jesus Himself was crucified because of the religious leaders' envy (Matt. 27:18). We can't fool ourselves into thinking that envy wouldn't take us down the same hate-filled road.

I'm sure that at some point you've felt the point of that knife poking at your ribs. We've all felt the stab that comes when someone else envies what we have. Here's the hard question we all have to answer: Do you ever wield it yourself?

When someone else gets a job promotion, recognition for an achievement, or even just a great haircut, do you rejoice with them or does the knife glint at your belt? Are you one that lifts your friend out of the bucket or a crab that pulls them down?

Our desires always lead us somewhere, whether it's to destruction or to the kingdom of God and His righteousness (Matt. 6:33). So, check yourself. Do you have crab claws today? If so, watch out. You may think that feeding envy will help you grab on to what you desire, but the enemy will use it to drag you down instead.

Resist envy as evidence that you trust the Lord and lay your desires at His feet. Express your faith that He will satisfy you by refusing to claw at the blessings He has given to others.

CONSIDER:

Is envy a sin you're guilty of today? How can you lift up or bless the person or group of people that you envy?

_____

_____

_____

_____

_____

_____

PRAY:

Tell God what you are desiring that tempts you to envy. Ask Him to give you a contented heart that is satisfied with Himself and His good provision.

TRUST:

Envy doesn't have to rule you. There's hope. Jesus is the Savior who came to deliver you from the destructive bents of your own heart.

> For we ourselves were once . . . slaves to various passions and pleasures, passing our days in malice and envy, hated by others and hating one another. But when the goodness and loving kindness of God our Savior appeared, he saved us. (Titus 3:3–5)

DO:

Choose someone whom you're tempted to envy. Rather than pulling them down, make an intentional choice to lift them up. Here are some ideas: You could post about them on social media, bless them with a small gift or a meal, set aside some time to pray for them, or just speak well of them to someone else.

DAY 3

Be kind to one another,
tenderhearted, forgiving one
another, as God in
Christ forgave you.

EPHESIANS 4:32

BE KIND TO *One Another,* FORGIVING *One Another*

Take every bitter thought you've ever held, and try to shape it into something useful. Go on. I'll wait right here.

Have your grudges led to good?

Has your bitterness made you better?

Has refusing to forgive made you feel free?

Of course not. We withhold forgiveness thinking doing so will give us relational power or place an impenetrable shield around our hurting hearts. And yet our power over the thoughts and actions of others remains limited and our hearts remain just as fragile. At the end of the day, our unforgiveness gains us nothing at all.

Paul warned us this was true in Ephesians 4.

"Now this I say, and testify in the Lord, that you must no longer walk as the Gentiles do, in the futility of their minds" (v. 17).

Did you catch the word he used to describe the thinking of the unbeliever? *Futile.* Meaning fruitless . . . useless . . . pointless. We can think withholding forgiveness is justified and worthwhile all we want, but which of your relationships have been restored through bitterness? Which hurts have mended by licking your wounds? How has your body been healed by allowing the acidity of unforgiveness to sink into your bones? Our lives reveal our bitterness to be futile—unproductive.

Paul offers us a better way to respond to one another.

"Be kind to one another, tenderhearted, forgiving one another, as God in Christ forgave you" (v. 32).

When the futility of unforgiveness isn't enough to motivate us to forgive the "one anothers" who hurt us, surely the gospel is. What a fruitful harvest Christ's forgiveness has produced! His kindness and grace has wooed us toward repentance (Rom. 2:4) and transformed our hearts of stone into hearts of flesh (Ezek. 11:19).

God will not bless your unforgiveness, but He can certainly use your choice to forgive. Every time you love the "one anothers" in your life this way, He is shaping you into a better image of Himself, a fruitful work indeed.

CONSIDER:

If bitterness and unforgiveness cannot move the needle toward peace in our relationships, why do we default to those two positions so often? What is it that we are secretly hoping to gain?

_____

_____

_____

_____

_____

_____

PRAY:

Ask God to help you adopt a zero tolerance policy toward unforgiveness. Invite Him to convict you immediately whenever you make the choice not to forgive and express your desire to mature away from futile ways of thinking in this area.

TRUST:

God is able to deal justly with your offenders. Entrust their care to Him rather than seeking to punish others through unforgiveness.

> For we know him who said, "Vengeance is mine; I will repay." And again, "The Lord will judge his people." (Hebrews 10:30)

DO:

Spend time considering Ephesians 1:3–14. Make a list of all that Christ's forgiveness has accomplished for you.

DAY 4

Clothe yourselves, all of you, with
humility toward one another, for
"God opposes the proud but gives
grace to the humble."

1 PETER 5:5

CLOTHE YOURSELVES WITH HUMILITY TOWARD *One Another*

It was the job no one wanted to do, but that hole in our front yard was the only chance of getting the septic field working again.

So, the workmen began executing their plan of attack. One man climbed down into the pit, filled with a ghastly mixture of mud and sludge, while the other helped him set up the equipment to snake it out.

Both men were covered with who knows what, but the man in the hole was up to his knees in it. Good thing he was wearing his overalls!

After hours of sweaty, backbreaking digging and pumping, they met their goal. Greg, my pastor, climbed out of the hole, and shared a warm, but dirty handshake with my dad, the software expert.

In that moment, they were no longer a preacher and a businessman. They were septic guys who had served my family well and gotten the job done.

They had taken off their suits and ties of honor and put on the work boots and denim of honest, humble labor. And in that moment, they reflected the humility of Jesus.

Peter had this picture in mind when he calls us to "clothe" ourselves with humility. In his day, slaves wore a particular garment that showed their role and status. Every day, when they tied on their white *enkomboma*, they were reminded of their station. And everyone around them immediately knew it, too—this person is a slave.

In the same way, when we wake up each day, we're to put on the garment of our calling as slaves of Jesus: humility.

It sounds simple, but *how* do we do this? It's not like we can pull a fresh, clean humility shirt out of our dressers each day.

John Henry Jowett, a pastor who ministered at the beginning of the twentieth century, gave some practical insight on this passage.

> Put on the apron of the slave! Go into the awful presence of the Lord, and contemplate His glory until the vision brings you wonderingly to your knees! "Go, stand on the mount before the Lord." That is the place where we discover our size! No man speaks of his greatness who has been closeted with God. Lordliness changes into holy fear, and pride bows down in reverent supplication. . . . It is the humble, kneeling soul that receives ineffable outpourings of Divine grace. Grace ever seeks out the lowliest.[1]

How do we put on our humility each day? In prayer! We take time to turn to the Lord, to remember that we are small and frail and sinful, and to tell Him that we need His strength, salvation, and forgiveness. And He promises to continue to give us grace for doing thankless jobs, enduring suffering, and loving others.

When this is our life's pattern, it will become as obvious as the clothing we wear—we're here, with humility wrapped around us, to do the work that needs to be done because we *are* the slaves of Jesus.

CONSIDER:

How can you practically put on humility each day? Is there a spiritual discipline or habit that would help you to see God's greatness and express your need for Him?

_____

_____

_____

_____

_____

_____

PRAY:

Take Pastor Jowett's advice and take time to think about and immerse yourself in God's greatness. Then tell Him how amazing He is either by praying or by singing a song that celebrates His glory.

TRUST:

Grace is available when we humble ourselves, and God truly cares for us. Hope is ahead, and today is not the end of the story.

> "God opposes the proud but gives grace to the humble." . . .
> [H]e cares for you. . . . And after you have suffered a little
> while, the God of all grace, who has called you to his eternal
> glory in Christ, will himself restore, confirm, strengthen, and
> establish you. (1 Peter 5:5, 7, 10)

DO:

Choose to practice humility today by doing something thankless or difficult for someone else. Look to God to give you grace to do it well and with love. He will help you.

DAY 5

Be filled with the Spirit . . .
submitting to one another out of
reverence for Christ.

EPHESIANS 5:18, 21

SUBMIT TO *One Another*

"I am the master of my fate, / I am the captain of my soul."[2]

This makes for great poetry, but not for wise living.

We often value the independent spirit, the person who can be decisive and "pull themselves up by their own bootstraps" and "not answer to any man." We see it as a strength to not need other people and to be our own masters. *But is this the way that God calls us to live?*

Check out today's verse. "Be filled with the Spirit . . . submitting to one another out of reverence for Christ" (Eph. 5:18, 21).

Submitting? To each other? To be honest, in my own heart of hearts, this often doesn't sound appealing. But it *is* one way that we can bear the image of Christ.

If we're following Jesus, we will walk like Jesus did, and *He submitted*.

- He submitted to His mom and earthly dad.
- He submitted to being baptized by His cousin John.
- He submitted in thousands of ways in the daily, nitty-gritty of being human and living with other humans.
- He submitted to His heavenly Father.
- He submitted to the cross.

As God, He was the only One who had any right to say, "I am the captain of my soul." But as Immanuel, the God-who-became-man, He instead humbled Himself, even to death on a cross.

No bootstraps. No fate-mastery. Only love demonstrated in humble submission.

If that was the way Jesus lived on this earth, why would we think self-sufficiency is a better way?

Our verse tells us that this submission flows out of fear of God. We want to walk in His ways. We want to please Him. We're fearful of wandering off the path. And so, we submit.

We submit to God's wisdom revealed in His Word. We submit to His direction in our lives. We willingly put ourselves under those God has appointed to lead us. And sometimes, out of fear of God, we yield to our brothers' and sisters' preferences rather than fall into sin by our own selfishness.

This isn't an easy path. It's not the way of immediate glory today, and likely there won't be a poem written in our lifetimes about how great our submission was. But there is glory waiting. God has exalted Jesus because of His submission, and He will turn *our* submission into something glorious at the end of days.

Though we make really crummy captains most of the time, *He* is the true Captain of our souls. And He will faithfully pilot us through the deeps as we walk together in submission.

CONSIDER:

Think of the people that God has called you to submit to—either because of their position or because of their close relationship to you. In what ways is God wanting you to submit more fully to them?

_____

_____

_____

_____

_____

_____

PRAY:

Take some time to pray for the people to whom you are called to submit. Ask the Lord to give you and them wisdom in your relationship.

TRUST:

Even when leaders are imperfect and fail, Jesus never does. We can submit because He is the perfect authority that will never fail or abandon His people.

> Remember your leaders, those who spoke to you the word of God. Consider the outcome of their way of life, and imitate their faith. Jesus Christ is the same yesterday and today and forever. (Hebrews 13:7-8)

DO:

Look up today's verse in your Bible, write it down, and post it somewhere that you can see it often until you have it memorized. Let God write the command of submitting to one another on your heart.

DAY 6

And let us consider how to
stir up one another to love
and good works.

HEBREWS 10:24

STIR UP *One Another* TO
LOVE AND GOOD WORKS

If we extract the command found in Hebrews 10:24 from the big idea surrounding it, the words feel a little small.

"And let us consider how to stir up one another to love and good works."

Without context this sounds like a reminder to drop a Hallmark card in the mail to someone you love. Perhaps a "thinking of you" or a "blessings on your day" would satisfy this command.

But look again. There is nothing small about what the writer of Hebrews is revealing.

> Therefore, brothers, since we have confidence to enter the holy places by the blood of Jesus, by the new and living way that he opened for us through the curtain, that is, through his flesh, and since we have a great priest over the house of God, let us draw near with a true heart in full assurance of faith, with our hearts sprinkled clean from an evil conscience and our bodies washed with pure water. Let us hold fast the confession of our hope without wavering, for he who promised is faithful. (vv. 19–23)

This is the gospel! The earthshaking, curtain-ripping, history-transforming gospel.

The writer is pointing us back to the Old Testament where the presence of God rested behind a curtain, inside the temple, inaccessible to all but a select few, and where atonement for sins required a constant, gory cycle.

Through His death, Christ secured our atonement once and for all, the curtain that separated us from Him was torn, and we are free to enter His presence with confidence.

Put that in a Hallmark card!

The "one anothers" command we find here in Hebrews 10 isn't a nudge toward niceties. It is a battle cry to remind each other of the gospel, to regularly point each other toward the bigness and goodness of God. The invitation is not simply to extend hope but *gospel hope* that fixates on the miraculous work of Christ for us, something we can't remind each other of too often.

So, consider this: how can you remind other believers of the gospel today? Use that question as your grid for what you say, send, and post.

CONSIDER:

Can you clearly articulate the gospel well enough to encourage others with it? If not, consider spending time reading Romans 3:23, 5:8, and 6:23.

_____

_____

_____

_____

_____

_____

PRAY:

Ask the Lord to give you opportunities this week to encourage other Christians with gospel hope.

TRUST:

The gospel is the hope we need most. It will do more to encourage your fellow Christ-followers than a pat on the back ever could.

> Let us hold fast the confession of our hope without wavering, for he who promised is faithful. (Hebrews 10:23)

DO:

Remind someone of the gospel today, and watch their spirits lift.

DAY 7

See that no one repays
anyone evil for evil, but always
seek to do good to one another
and to everyone.

1 THESSALONIANS 5:15

ALWAYS SEEK TO DO GOOD
TO *One Another*

"Hello! My name is Inigo Montoya. You killed my father. Prepare to die."

This famous line is uttered at the climax of the film *The Princess Bride*. In the movie, the character Inigo has spent his entire life seeking vengeance for his father's murder. He finally catches up with the object of his hatred, Count Rugen. After a dramatic sword battle, Inigo finally begins making demands.

"Offer me money. Power, too."

The Count desperately makes promises—he'll give Inigo anything he wants, if he will spare his life.

But at the end, nothing can satisfy the Spaniard's desire for revenge. "I want my father back," Inigo declares, as he runs Rugen through with his sword.

In the end, he gets his vengeance . . . Count Rugen is dead. But even that cannot bring Inigo's father back to him. Having completed his life goal, with nothing but blood on his hands to show for it, Inigo reflects on his loss of purpose. What do you do when you're "no longer in the revenge business"?

In the end, there's nothing left but piracy. He's doomed to a life of wandering the seas aimlessly, pursuing temporary wealth at others' expense. He has become so wrapped up in his desires, on his self-focused pursuit of getting what he wants, that nothing but *more* blood and riches and glory can appeal to him. He's doomed to a life of more of the same, alone and hidden behind a mask.

What is the definition of a wasted and lonely life, after all, but a life focused on revenge?

Few, if any, of us are trying to avenge a murder. But there's smaller, subtler ways that we can try to get even and separate ourselves from others who hurt us. Backstabbing, ignoring, gossiping, quietly undermining . . . they come from a heart turned toward vengeance rather than love.

First Thessalonians 5:15 offers us a better way, a way that builds relationships rather than tearing them down: give up revenge and pursue doing good. The way to deal with our self-centered tendencies is not just to hold our tongues and lift our eyes to heaven in frustration (though that can be part of it!); it's to go a step further.

The verse before (v. 14) says, "admonish the idle, encourage the fainthearted, help the weak, be patient with them all." The Holy Spirit was purposeful in guiding the apostle's pen. We can be sure there's a reason why the warning against revenge and the command to chase after blessing others follows this verse.

Perhaps it means that . . .

- The people who seem lazy
- The people who are always "down" or anxious
- The people who always need your help
- The people who try your patience
- The people who hurt you

. . . they're the exact people God wants you to bless.

That may seem impossible, but isn't this what Jesus did for us? "He did not open his mouth" (Isa. 53:7 CSB) or pull out a sword as He was led away to be crucified, but instead He said, "Father, forgive them" (Luke 23:34). He sought God's blessing of mercy for us, His betrayers.

Our Savior has given us grace to do the same. So by doing good, let's put down our weapons and our piercing words. Vengeance won't satisfy us anyway.

CONSIDER:

Do you take up vengeance in small ways? Against whom?

_____

_____

_____

_____

_____

_____

PRAY:

If you had an answer to the question above, confess it to the Lord, and ask Him for grace to do good to those people. Then take a moment to pray for them.

TRUST:

Your obedience to this command doesn't mean that person gets off the hook. God will repay justly, in His way and His time.

> Beloved, never avenge yourselves, but leave it to the wrath of God, for it is written, "Vengeance is mine, I will repay, says the Lord." (Romans 12:19)

DO:

Intentionally look for some way to bless someone who annoys, frustrates, or hurts you—and do it without delay. (If you can't think of anything, ask the Lord to bless that person and show you if there's a way He wants to use you to bless them.)

PART II:
Your Presence

"They shall call his name Immanuel"
(which means, God with us).

MATTHEW 1:23

"I will not leave you as orphans;
I will come to you."

JOHN 14:18

"Behold, I am with you always,
to the end of the age."

MATTHEW 28:20

DAY 8

Welcome one another as
Christ has welcomed you,
for the glory of God.

ROMANS 15:7

WELCOME *One Another*

In a town that I lived in several years ago, there was a doughnut shop infamous for *not* serving people. With signs posted on the wall of their establishment, the owners made it clear that certain people— essentially anyone different than them—were not welcome.

These businesspeople showed that they looked only at the outward appearance. They would not get close enough to *see* the doughnut-lover across the counter. Because, after all, they were only (fill in the pejorative term here), not customers to be served or God's image-bearers to be loved.

Maybe we don't have signs posted on our front doors or on our chests saying, "____ not welcome here." So, it's easy to hear a story like that and think, *Those people* . . . But when I look at my own heart, it doesn't take long to realize: those same signs hang on the walls of my heart.

- I look across the table at a Christian brother or sister that I don't easily relate to and wish I was elsewhere.
- I run into someone who thinks differently on an issue, and my mind quickly jumps to judging them. Or I get angry at the person *and* their position.
- In my more petty moments, I take joy in the fact that I feel free to do something because I know it would make another believer uncomfortable.

My heart's not a pretty picture. At times I wish I didn't have to deal with differences. Resting in the safety of "sameness" feels much easier. It definitely takes a lot less effort and sacrifice.

If this is you, too, our verse for today has something to teach us.

Paul wrote those words to a church that was in conflict because of differences. (Read Romans 14:1–15:7 to see what they were.) When you put believers from a Jewish background who have a specific way of doing things with believers from a Gentile background who have their own way of doing things . . . without love, things blow up. Names get called. Judgment happens. Quarreling becomes a way of life.

Paul reminds us that the way to love one another in the moments we'd like to kick our fellow Christians out of the doughnut shop is to instead *welcome* them.

My Greek dictionary tells me that "welcoming" means to take that person to yourself, to let that person into your heart as a friend. It's not just doing your Christian duty of handing someone a bulletin at the door of the church with a smile and then never talking to them again. It looks more like inviting them to your home, welcoming them into your life, and accepting them as an equal member of God's family, as Jesus accepted you.

That person? *That* welcome in your life?

Isn't that what Jesus has done for us? When we were the ones who were outside His family and alienated from His covenant, He brought us to Himself and into His family by His blood (Eph. 2:11–13, 19).

So, as we walk in this mercy, let's "live in . . . harmony with one another" and sing "with one voice . . . for the glory of God" (Rom. 15:5–7). How? It starts with resting in the truth that we, ourselves, have been accepted, and it continues by extending that same welcome to our brothers and sisters.

Will you join me? If so, I hear that doughnuts are a great way to make new friends.

CONSIDER:

Who are the people you know that you'd rather not get to know better? How could you consciously welcome them into your life?

_____

_____

_____

_____

_____

_____

PRAY:

Thank God for welcoming and accepting you into His family, and ask Him to give you that same heart for others.

TRUST:

He will give you wisdom to navigate differences in the Church, and He will welcome *you* into His presence one day.

> You guide me with your counsel, and afterward you will receive me to glory. (Psalm 73:24)

DO:

This week, find a small way to extend friendship to a believer who is different from you, whether it's by simply striking up a conversation or by inviting them over for coffee and doughnuts. Get it on the calendar, and then ask the Lord to help you to carefully listen to and enjoy them as a sibling in Christ.

DAY 9

Comfort one another . . . and the
God of love and peace
will be with you.

2 CORINTHIANS 13:11

COMFORT *One Another*

I've lost track of how many funerals I've been to.

Between the ages of nine and eighteen, I went to the funerals of five of my grandparents and a great aunt. It was a difficult season for my family, to say the least. A couple of the deaths were sudden—but most were preceded by long declines.

In each situation, the pain was acute. I watched my parents weep as they said goodbye to parents and grandparents. I helped as I could by sorting through possessions and watching younger siblings during hospital visits. I recall holidays with moments of grief, as we remembered that the person who held up a tradition was no longer with us. Each person who died, even the ones with whom we had rocky relationships, left an unfillable hole.

Why do I tell you all this? Because I know that you have experienced, or will experience, loss, too. And God can use your grief like He has used mine.

In high school, after many of these deaths, two of my best friends lost grandparents very suddenly. I happened to be reading 2 Corinthians at the time and ran across these verses:

> Blessed be the God and Father of our Lord Jesus Christ, the Father of mercies and God of all comfort, who comforts us in all our affliction, so that we may be able to comfort those who are in any affliction, with the comfort with which we ourselves are comforted by God. (1:3–4)

I realized that all the losses, all the funerals, and all the tears that I had questioned God about, they had a purpose for *this* moment. The Lord led me through all that grief so I could be there for my friends in a way I wouldn't have otherwise.

That has proven true into adulthood. As friends have lost loved ones, God has often given me wisdom about what's needed in a moment of grief, a comforting truth to share, and an ability to listen and understand because I've walked through the valley of the shadow of death. The God of all comfort has allowed His comfort to pass through me in a way that is only explained by this verse.

He is merciful. He is sovereign. He is good.

Each moment of pain that you walk through, each funeral you attend, is an opportunity to run to the heart of your Father and receive His comfort. Every moment of pain you encounter in others' lives is an opportunity to give that same comfort to them.

Your suffering is a commission. When you experience the effects of being in a broken world and turn to the Lord with your pain, you're made into a messenger of mercy, hope, and comfort. God gives it to you; you give it to others.

When you have a list of griefs and losses that you cannot count, look around you. There may be someone in the pew next to you or living next door who could use some comfort. And maybe you're the one God has chosen to do just that.

CONSIDER:

What experiences or suffering do you have available for God to use?
Is there anyone around you who is dealing with similar issues? How could
you give them comfort?

_____

_____

_____

PRAY:

Ask the Lord to use your circumstances in life, past or present, to bless
someone else. If there are people you know who are suffering, take some
time to pray the same for them.

TRUST:

Your suffering is not the end of the story. God is in the business of
exchanging our sorrows for joy and glorifying Himself through our lives.

> The Spirit of the Lord God is upon me,
> because the Lord has anointed me
> to bring good news to the poor;
> he has sent me to bind up the brokenhearted . . .
> to give them a beautiful headdress instead of ashes,
> the oil of gladness instead of mourning,
> the garment of praise instead of a faint spirit;
> that they may be called oaks of righteousness,
> the planting of the Lord, that he may be glorified. (Isaiah 61:1, 3)

DO:

If you personally know someone who is suffering, show them the comfort
of Christ in a small way today. If you don't know what is helpful, ask.
Often just knowing that someone cares can be a comfort in itself!

DAY 10

Bear one another's burdens,
and so fulfill the law of Christ.

GALATIANS 6:2

BEAR *One Another's* BURDENS

I remember the day that I got the mysterious envelope. No return address; no clues as to who it was from. Inside was an anonymous cashier's check for exactly what I still needed to pay for my college tuition that semester.

I had been praying hard, because I had no idea how I was going to come up with the needed funds. But somehow, without me mentioning it, someone in my life found out that I needed some burden lifting. I never found out who it was . . . but I've continued to be grateful for that person and their gift.

Many times in my life, I've been the recipient of such a gift from an unknown source. There was the $500 someone gave to the deacons at my church to help me purchase a car. Once someone slipped some cash onto my desk when I was feeling unstable financially. Another time I was handed a check by a complete stranger to support my ministry work.

There have also been the gifts that were not anonymous but quiet. The long hours that friends have spent listening to my sorrows, my parents' tendency to quietly slip money into my bank account so I can visit home, the many times I've been fed by families in my church when I couldn't return the favor, the room offered to me by friends so I wouldn't have to live alone . . . these people have all helped to bear my burdens. And by so doing, they've fulfilled Christ's law.

What is that law? It's the law of love. "Love does no wrong to a neighbor; therefore love is the fulfilling of the law" (Rom. 13:10).

It means that when someone we know is struggling, whether it is financially or emotionally or even with sin, our job is not to lay heavier weights of guilt, shame, or rules on them but to help relieve their burden. It's to come alongside them, like Jesus does for us, and help them carry the load with gentleness. When we do this, we "really fulfill the royal law according to the Scripture, 'You shall love your neighbor as yourself'" (James 2:8).

Perhaps bearing someone's burdens will mean coming alongside them as a friend, or it may mean pulling out your wallet and sharing what you have without recognition.

No one gives Nobel Peace Prizes to the family who practices hospitality every Sunday or an MVP trophy to the person who entertains a stressed mom's kids for a few hours or an Oscar to the one who anonymously pays for someone else's groceries. But these are the actions that Jesus rewards. He sees, and by doing this work you live out His love in a way that is tangible, eternally lasting, and glorifying to Him.

CONSIDER:

How can you bear someone else's burden today? Is there a hurting friend you can reach out to, a family you can financially help, or someone lonely you can invite over?

_____

_____

_____

PRAY:

Let the words of this prayer by Francis of Assisi guide you in asking the Lord to help you know how to bear others' burdens:

> O Master, let me not seek as much
> to be consoled as to console,
> to be understood as to understand,
> to be loved as to love,
> for it is in giving that one receives,
> it is in self-forgetting that one finds,
> it is in pardoning that one is pardoned,
> it is in dying that one is raised to eternal life.

TRUST:

As you bear others' burdens in obedience, Christ will help bear yours and give you rest.

> "Come to me, all who labor and are heavy laden, and I will give you rest. Take my yoke upon you, and learn from me, for I am gentle and lowly in heart, and you will find rest for your souls. For my yoke is easy, and my burden is light." (Matthew 11:28–30)

DO:

The first thing to do today is to pray. Pray for the people you know who are bearing heavy burdens, and ask the Lord to give you an idea of how to help one of them. Then do as He prompts you and help carry that person's load in a practical way. Perhaps try one of the ways I wrote about in today's devotional if someone specific came to mind as you read.

DAY 11

I therefore, a prisoner for the
Lord, urge you to walk in a
manner worthy of the calling
to which you have been called,
with all humility and gentleness,
with patience, bearing with one
another in love.

EPHESIANS 4:1–2

BEAR WITH *One Another*
IN LOVE

Forbearance.

It's an old-fashioned word and, in many ways, an out-of-date idea.

Forbearance is patience that lasts more than a moment. It's sticking with someone in their struggle and holding back our anger, annoyance, or hurt for the long haul, maybe days, weeks, or years. Maybe even a lifetime.

We're not a forbearant culture. We expect people to get their acts together, and fast. If they cannot, or will not, we feel justified in losing faith in them. God's Word calls us to a different way.

Take a peek at Ephesians 4:1, which says, "I therefore, a prisoner for the Lord, urge you to walk in a manner worthy of the calling to which you have been called."

This is the umbrella command Paul is giving the followers of Christ. The big idea is that while we cannot live in a way that earns our status as ambassadors for Jesus, we can, by the power of the Holy Spirit, live lives worthy of such an honorable calling.

I know what you're thinking. I'm thinking it too. *How?* How can I, a sinner through and through, live a life worthy of the call of Christ? For starters, I can choose forbearance toward my fellow ambassadors.

If "walk in a manner worthy of the calling" is the umbrella, "bearing with one another in love" (v. 2) is the handle. It gives us something to hold on to, a practical way to live worthy of our calling.

Are we ever more like God than when we bear with one another?

After all, we "are justified by his grace as a gift, through the redemption that is in Christ Jesus, whom God put forward as a propitiation by his blood, to be received in faith. *This was to show God's righteousness, because in his divine forbearance he had passed over former sins*" (Rom. 3:24–25).

In our sin, in our struggle, Christ bears with us. He refuses to throw in the towel whether we miss the mark once or a million times. How can we live lives worthy of His divine patience? By bearing with one another. That's an idea worth bringing back in style.

CONSIDER:

Is there someone that you've given up on? Ask God to show you how to bear with them instead.

_____

_____

PRAY:

Make Psalm 103:8–14 your prayer.

> The LORD is merciful and gracious,
> slow to anger and abounding in steadfast love.
> He will not always chide,
> nor will he keep his anger forever.
> He does not deal with us according to our sins,
> nor repay us according to our iniquities.
> For as high as the heavens are above the earth,
> so great is his steadfast love toward those who fear him;
> as far as the east is from the west,
> so far does he remove our transgressions from us.
> As a father shows compassion to his children,
> so the LORD shows compassion to those who fear him.
> For he knows our frame; he remembers that we are dust.

TRUST:

As you bear with the shortcomings of others, Christ is bearing with your weakness, too.

> The LORD passed before him and proclaimed, "The LORD,
> the LORD, a God merciful and gracious, slow to anger, and
> abounding in steadfast love and faithfulness." (Exodus 34:6)

DO:

Relieve someone of your expectations today. You don't have to verbalize it, but in your heart, commit to sticking with your spouse, your children, your coworkers, or your friends, and continue to show love even if they struggle.

DAY 12

Be kind to one another,
tenderhearted, forgiving
one another, as God in Christ
forgave you.

EPHESIANS 4:32

BE KIND TO *One Another*

You pour yourself a nice hot cup of coffee, pour some milk in to take the bitter edge off, grab your phone or newspaper, and settle in for a quick moment of reset before the day starts.

Can you picture it? Birds chirping outdoors, sun just glancing over the hill across the street.

Then . . . you take the first sip—and spit it right back out. Ugh! *What was the date on that milk?*

That kind of experience lingers. It's really hard to get rid of the taste, and even harder to get rid of the memory. Worst case, it ruins coffee altogether for you for a while.

That kind of sourness is exactly what happens when there's a lack of kindness in the Body of Christ. When we respond to our brothers and sisters with harshness, a lack of compassion, and bitterness, we have a similar effect on others as when we drink curdled milk in a latte. We leave a horrible taste in their mouths.

We want to be life-givers. We want to nourish those around us, not to make them want to vomit us out like the fish did to Jonah.

But the fact is we're sinners. We're going to be unkind at times, and though the Spirit will grow us in kindness, we're going to fail.

Is there any hope? Yes.

Did you know that curdled milk can be used by a skilled gardener to promote plant growth or a knowledgeable baker in various ways? Though our first instinct may be to throw that milk out, never to be seen again, it *can* be used. There just has to be someone skilled, capable, and willing to stay in it to the end who can put it to good use.

Praise God that He is just that sort of Savior. He is able "to present you blameless before the presence of his glory" (Jude 24). He will bring His "good work in you . . . to completion" (Phil. 1:6).

When you find yourself in a pit of bitterness, repenting again, or responding to a family member in harsh frustration, *the gospel is for you.* If we confess our sins, He promises to forgive and when we're tempted to be unkind, He promises to help us (1 John 1:9; Heb. 4:16). That's good news!

And miracles of miracles, He doesn't just *use* sour milk, He transforms it. We might see ourselves as spoiled and beyond help—or see our neighbors that way—but for those who have been saved, there is hope. We are becoming fresh, useful, and life-giving again by the Spirit of our God (1 Cor. 6:11).

CONSIDER:

Were your interactions with others today and yesterday kind or sour? How would those around you describe your words and attitude toward them? How would you describe your thoughts in those moments?

_____

_____

_____

PRAY:

Confess any unkindness that the Lord has revealed to you, and ask God to do the miracle of transforming you and making you useful in bringing life, hope, and joy to others.

TRUST:

God is transforming us by showing us His glory day by day. His Spirit is making us new.

> And we all, with unveiled face, beholding the glory of the Lord, are being transformed into the same image from one degree of glory to another. For this comes from the Lord who is the Spirit. (2 Corinthians 3:18)

DO:

Make a list of ways that you can show small, everyday kindness to those around you. Then choose just one and make it happen today.

PART III:

Your Communication

Let me hear what God the LORD
will speak, for he will speak peace to
his people, to his saints.

PSALM 85:8

Jesus, looking at him, loved him, and said . . .

MARK 10:21

DAY 13

Do not lie to one another, seeing
that you have put off the old self
with its practices.

COLOSSIANS 3:9

DO NOT LIE TO *One Another*

· ·

"Where are you?"

These were God's first words to Adam and Eve after they ate the forbidden fruit. Did God need to be told this? Of course not. But He knew that *they* needed to be honest. They needed to acknowledge that they were in a place they weren't meant to be. They needed to act out of faith that God was in charge by speaking the truth.

Does it seem like I'm reading too much into the Genesis 3 account? If so, take a look at the passage today's verse comes from. Paul writes:

> If then you have been raised with Christ, seek the things that are above, where Christ is, seated at the right hand of God. Set your minds on things that are above, not on things that are on earth. For you have died, and your life is hidden with Christ in God. When Christ who is your life appears, then you also will appear with him in glory. (Col. 3:1-4)

He's laying out these truths: Our salvation is a reason to chase after and look toward the eternal—Christ Himself and His kingdom. Our old self that loves today's treasures has died. We have new life in Jesus now, and we're destined for glory.

Then the apostle continues:

> Put to death therefore what is earthly in you. . . . Do not lie to one another, seeing that you have put off the old self with its practices and have put on the new self. (vv. 5, 9-10)

When we hide ourselves like our first parents—when we refrain from speaking the truth about our lives—we are living like our old, dead selves, not as resurrected, new creations. Like Adam and Eve, we're picking the fruit that's right in front of us instead of trusting God to provide for us and know what's best for us.

Telling the truth about a situation or an aspect of your life can be really costly, it's true. It may cost you a job or a relationship or social status. But those things are not our primary source of identity anymore.

> You have been raised with Christ. . . . For you have died.
> . . . Here there is not Greek and Jew, circumcised and
> uncircumcised, barbarian, Scythian, slave, free; but Christ is
> all, and in all. (vv. 1, 3, 11)

Your social standing or vocational position are no longer something to hold on to for dear life. Christ is. And Christ is worth everything. *Christ is worth speaking the truth.*

Each time we choose to be honest with those around us, we're demonstrating that we trust in Someone beyond what we can see. We're living out of faith that our good Christ and sovereign God will work out what's best for us as we live with integrity—even if everything else we're holding on to from this earthly life is stripped away.

Stop hiding. Stop lying. Believe that He cares for you when you obediently speak the truth. Today He gently invites you to Himself with this question: "Where are you?" Tell Him. And then tell someone else.

CONSIDER:

Where are you? Is there anything you're hiding from others out of fear? Are there any ways you've been walking in deceit rather than integrity?

_____

_____

_____

PRAY:

Tell the Lord exactly where you are. Are you angry? Tell Him. Are you walking in sin? Confess to Him. Are you longing for something that you haven't spoken aloud? Share that with Him.

TRUST:

God provides mercy when we are honest about where we are. He forgives when we confess our sins. He provides grace for sharing the truth with others.

> Whoever conceals his transgressions will not prosper, but he who confesses and forsakes them will obtain mercy. (Proverbs 28:13)

DO:

Let someone see where you actually are this week. Find a wise person who can walk with you personally, and invite them in to see the reality of your life. Speak the truth to them, let them ask you hard questions, and receive the gift of their input.

DAY 14

Therefore, confess your sins to
one another and pray for one
another, that you may be healed.

JAMES 5:16

CONFESS YOUR SINS TO
One Another

One of my best purchases ever was a weighted blanket.

It stays permanently on my bed to provide a sense of safety and security in the evening hours. It's a gift that I'm thankful for—because it does what it was designed to do.

Now imagine if I got so attached to that blanket that I carried it around everywhere. I'd probably lose a few pounds with the effort (it's heavy!), but it would keep me from moving freely. Every step would be a burden. I'd stop doing some of my favorite things. Playing the piano is pretty impossible if you can't raise your arms. Hugging my loved ones, cooking, and even getting a book off the shelf would become a burden.

Likely, I'd stop being as social, out of love for the blanket. People in my life would get pushed away because I'd be embarrassed by being continually wrapped up like a child and because I wouldn't want to get worn out by the weight on me. And there are the consequences of having people close to me. Maybe someone would call me out about it. Maybe I'd have to give it up. Maybe I'd be made fun of. *Nope. I'll just stay in bed with this cozy blanket. It's much safer.*

Isn't this just how we are sometimes with our sin? Here's a truth that we may want to ignore: sin often makes us feel cozy. Like my "security blanket," our sin can provide a sense of safety. We can easily trick our minds and hearts into thinking that we're safer hiding under our sin. Giving it up, confessing it, admitting to someone that we need help? *Um . . . I'll just stay here where it's safe.*

Sin isn't a weight that we're meant to carry around. It's supposed to be left in one place, at the cross of Jesus.

But sometimes, we need the help of others in getting to Him. That's why James told us to "confess your sins to one another and pray for one another, that you may be healed."

My blanket, as great as it is, isn't a substitute for real-life interactions with people I love and actual physical touch. Sometimes what I really need is a sister-friend to let me cry on their shoulder or a hug from someone who cares and will point me to Jesus. In the same way, the pseudo-safety of hiding in our sin doesn't replace the joy for being really known and cared for and prayed for.

The weight of our sin, by default, pushes us away from godly intimacy with others. We wrap ourselves in shame and fear—and we keep ourselves from the healing that God desires to give us through confession. God designs us with a need for each other. And that kind of intimacy often requires vulnerability that often feels costly.

What are you wrapping yourself in today? Is it the forgiveness of God and the prayers of others . . . or the weight of your sin? There's freedom available, but you have to be willing to put down the blanket.

CONSIDER:

What weights are you needing to put down? Are you wrapping yourself in the "safety" of anything that God wants to take from you?

_____

_____

_____

PRAY:

> Search me, O God, and know my heart!
> Try me and know my thoughts!
> And see if there be any grievous way in me,
> and lead me in the way everlasting! (Psalm 139:23–24)

Then confess whatever He reveals, and ask Him for grace to walk in the way He leads.

TRUST:

Opening up to other believers about your sins and sorrows is one of the means God uses for your healing. Having their prayers matters.

> Confess your sins to one another and pray for one another,
> that you may be healed. The prayer of a righteous person
> has great power as it is working. (James 5:16)

DO:

Grab another believer and pray with them. Ask how they need prayer, and share honestly about your needs. Then take those needs to God together.

DAY 15

Live in harmony with one another.

ROMANS 12:16

LIVE IN HARMONY WITH
One Another

. . . .

Scripture poses a very important question. For the
Christ-follower, it is *the* question our lives hinge upon . . .

"How should we then live?" (Ezek. 33:10 KJV).

In light of all that Christ has done for us . . .
In gratitude for the ways He has transformed us . . .
Because He has promised to return for us . . .

How should we then live?

God doesn't leave us guessing. The pages of the Bible are filled with
instructions for how to live in light of God's Truth. Take for example,
the apostle Paul's words recorded in Romans 12:9–21. While the earlier
chapters of Romans are dedicated to clearly outlining the gospel, here,
Paul gets down to the brass tacks of how the gospel transforms our
everyday lives. In the margin of my Bible beside these verses, I've written
the words "marching orders" along with a list of the specific actions the
Bible is asking me to take.

Take a moment and do the same. In the margin of your Bible, or a
separate sheet of paper, list the "marching orders" you see in Romans
12:9–21.

Several "one anothers" made the list. There's "love one another with
brotherly affection" (v. 10), "outdo one another in showing honor" (v. 10),
and finally, "live in harmony with one another" (v. 16).

Let's drill down on that third command for a moment.

Harmony—it's a musical term that refers to a pleasing arrangement of parts. Harmony cannot come from a single note, even an exceptionally beautiful one. Harmony only happens when multiple notes are arranged together to create a seamless sound.

Since the gospel transforms us from sinners in need of a Savior to saints fully accepted by God, how should we then live?

In harmony, laying aside our rights, our preferences, and our frustrations to live at peace with our brothers and sisters in Christ. When we do, our lives join together in a single song, declaring the wonder of God's grace.

CONSIDER:

Who do you struggle most to live with in harmony? How does this division impact your gospel witness?

_____

_____

_____

PRAY:

Ask the Lord to help you to live in harmony with others. Repent for the ways you have contributed to discord.

TRUST:

A day is coming when God's children will live in perfect peace.

> My people will abide in a peaceful habitation,
> in secure dwellings, and in quiet resting places. (Isaiah 32:18)

DO:

Commit to contributing to harmony within God's Church.

DAY 16

Let us not become conceited,
provoking one another,
envying one another.

GALATIANS 5:26

LET US NOT PROVOKE
One Another

"Mom, she's touching me!"

"I'm *not* touching you!" Her finger poked in the air near her sister.

"But you're being annoooyyyyying! Mom!"

"But I'm not *touching you!*" The sing-song voice simply provoked the other child more.

A familiar voice finally rang out, "You guys are doing a backflip on my last nerve!"

(This may or may not have happened in real life. I'll leave you to guess which kid I was.)

If you're a parent or someone who spends a lot of time with children, this is likely a familiar scene. One child gets bored or frustrated, or just curious, and finds some way to test the boundaries. *How much can I irritate my sibling? Which of Mom or Dad's buttons can I push?* And their proverbial finger (or their literal one!) goes out to poke and prod and irritate.

Chaos ensues, and usually it ends with an exasperated adult and protesting children, often both.

It happens to adults, too. We're more subtle about it to be sure, but those same tendencies can be there to intentionally bring the worst out of others. Maybe it's through manipulation or being passive-aggressive or not acknowledging someone else's contributions. We seek ourselves and our glory . . . and often that ends in conflict and broken relationships.

Why do scenes like this happen? Galatians 5 tells us—it's because we "gratify the desires of the flesh" (v. 16), which causes us to be selfish glory hogs that enjoy pushing each other's buttons because we want what each other has.

How do we change the pattern of our lives from that of provoking each other this way to provoking one another "to love and good works" (Heb. 10:24)? I have good news and bad news.

The bad news is that *we* can't. In ourselves, we can't change our hearts. We might be able to modify our behavior, but deep down we'd continue to be provocateurs of all that's terrible in others' hearts. Our hearts go that direction, even if the mask on the outside doesn't.

The good news is *God* can change us. His Holy Spirit can turn us from provoking to loving. He can bring His fruit out of us, as we rely on Him. Only He can produce love, joy, peace, patience, kindness, goodness, faithfulness, gentleness, and self-control in our relationships (Gal. 5:22–23).

When we're tempted to be the little child poking our brother or sister, what do we do? We turn to God, our loving parent, and cry out for help. He doesn't have a last nerve and won't get exasperated or angry. He will give you grace to love rather than provoke those around you.

CONSIDER:

Who are the people in your life that you can most easily provoke? What are some ways you could provoke them toward love and good works rather than frustration?

_____

_____

_____

PRAY:

Consider your closest relationships, and ask God to produce His fruit in you as you live life with them. Confess the ways that you tend to provoke them, and cry out to Him to transform your heart.

TRUST:

As you hold fast to the Word of God and seek His face, the Lord will grow the seeds of the gospel up into good fruit. Be patient.

> "A sower went out to sow his seed. . . . And some fell into good soil and grew and yielded a hundredfold. . . . As for that in the good soil, they are those who, hearing the word, hold it fast in an honest and good heart, and bear fruit with patience." (Luke 8:5, 8, 15)

DO:

If the Lord has convicted you of being provoking in the wrong way, go to those you have irritated and ask their forgiveness. And if they're a believer, ask them to pray for you about this, too.

DAY 17

Do not speak evil against
one another, brothers.

JAMES 4:11

DO NOT SPEAK EVIL AGAINST
One Another

· ·

There are days I need a whistle.

As the mother of four sons, I referee a lot of fights. So many that some days I feel like the referee in an NFL football game, constantly throwing a flag on the play and then listening as each boy takes his turn verbally replaying how they've been wronged.

It's not a boy problem or a kid problem. It's a human problem. We're all prone to go on the defensive when the people in our home, church, and workplace don't do what we want them to do.

Once sin entered the lives of mankind, it didn't take long for us to turn on each other. Within a single generation of Adam and Eve's original sin, their children were fighting over who mattered more. That particular dispute ended very badly (Gen. 4:1–16), but it didn't start with physical violence. It started with a war of words.

"Cain spoke to Abel his brother" (v. 8).

Cain and Abel are the poster children for a harsh reality; *murder begins with words.*

Jesus confirmed this when He said, "You have heard that it was said to those of old, 'You shall not murder; and whoever murders will be liable to judgment.' But I say to you that everyone who is angry with his brother will be liable to judgment; whoever insults his brother will be liable to the council; and whoever says, 'You fool!' will be liable to the hell of fire'" (Matt. 5:21–22).

We may draw the line for sin at murder and feel smug that we've never crossed it, but Jesus, it seems, is not as impressed as we might hope. As we live as His ambassadors (2 Cor. 5:20), He commands us to avoid warring with words.

Imagine if someone had stepped in between Cain and Abel and spoken the straightforward words recorded in James 4:11: "Do not speak evil against one another, brothers." Imagine if they'd listened.

If the brothers had refused to speak ill of each other, their conflict would have diffused. Cain would not carry the guilt of his brother's death, Abel would live the life God intended for him, and unity would be restored.

There are times we all feel like our lives have become a gridiron. We yell at each other on social media and send passive aggressive stares across our dining room tables. We fight with those we love the most and go to war with the strangers who dare to pass us in the wrong lane as we commute. God chooses not to referee every fight between His children. He isn't in the business of blowing the whistle every time we're at odds. Instead, He warns us to cut off the conflict at the place it begins—with our words.

You cannot choose how other people will behave today. You cannot change the heart of a single other human. But you can avoid Cain's mistake by living out this simple command: "Do not speak evil against one another."

CONSIDER:

How does talking about an offense give life to hurt, anger, or resentment? In contrast, what happens if we don't verbalize when we feel wronged?

_____

_____

_____

PRAY:

Make Psalm 141:3 your prayer today (and every day!).

> Set a guard, O Lord, over my mouth;
> keep watch over the door of my lips! (Psalm 141:3)

TRUST:

God is at work to transform your heart, which *will* impact the way that you talk.

> "It is not what goes into the mouth that defiles a person,
> but what comes out of the mouth; this defiles a person."
> (Matthew 15:11)

DO:

Memorize James 4:11, and repeat it when you face the temptation to speak words intended to harm another person.

DAY 18

Do not grumble against one
another, brothers, so that you
may not be judged; behold, the
Judge is standing at the door.

JAMES 5:9

DO NOT GRUMBLE AGAINST
One Another

. . . .

How do you treat others when your patience has worn thin? That's the hard question Scripture asks us to wrestle to the ground in James 5.

As we wait for Christ's return, how do we talk to those who wait alongside us? Do we patiently endure the suffering that comes with living in a broken world with grace, or do we, instead, become irritable, and take our angst out on the "one anothers" all around us? Do our words communicate confidence in the Lord's imminent return, or do they betray the truth that our hearts have grown faint in the waiting?

"Do not grumble against one another, brothers, so that you may not be judged; behold, the Judge is standing at the door" (v. 9).

On a smaller scale, how do you treat others in seasons of personal suffering? When life is hard, do you lash out? Place blame? Justify sharp and hurtful words? What we say is not disconnected from what we believe. Scripture warns us that our words reveal the true condition of our hearts. "The good person out of the good treasure of his heart produces good, and the evil person out of his evil treasure produces evil, for out of the abundance of the heart his mouth speaks" (Luke 6:45).

Who we are in times of trial is who we are. Suffering will continue to come in waves until Christ returns for us. When those waves roll us over, and we find ourselves gasping for breath, for hope, our true heart for the "one anothers" is revealed.

God's Word nudges us to endure suffering with quiet patience, like a farmer waiting to see evidence of his crop emerge from the ground

(James 5:7). Patience is a virtue that pays big dividends in our relationships with one another. Patience is possible, not because of our confidence in the "one anothers" we wait beside but because of our confidence in Christ.

"You also, be patient. Establish your hearts, for the coming of the Lord is at hand" (v. 8).

When we choose to respond to one another with grace, we are declaring our hope in the Lord's coming.

When we refuse to turn against one another and choose to endure with quiet patience, we are declaring our hope in the Lord's coming.

When we speak words of life instead of grumbling against the image-bearers of God, we are declaring our hope in the Lord's coming.

If you find yourself grumbling in these difficult days, don't look to the "one anothers" for relief. Look to Christ. Ask Him to renew your hope in His return so that out of your mouth flow words of life.

CONSIDER:

How does regularly considering the return of Christ practically impact the way we view our suffering?

_____

_____

_____

PRAY:

Ask the Lord to reveal how your words expose weak faith. Repent for lashing out at others in times of suffering.

TRUST:

God's grace is sufficient to help you live a godly life as you wait for His return.

> For the grace of God has appeared, bringing salvation for all people, training us to renounce ungodliness and worldly passions, and to live self-controlled, upright, and godly lives in the present age, waiting for our blessed hope, the appearing of the glory of our great God and Savior Jesus Christ. (Titus 2:11–13)

DO:

Meditate on 1 Thessalonians 4:16–17, focusing on the wonder of Christ's return.

DAY 19

Therefore, confess your sins to
one another and pray for one
another, that you may be healed.
The prayer of a righteous person
has great power as it is working.

JAMES 5:16

PRAY FOR *One Another*

. . . .

If it wasn't for Dree, I might still be sitting on the airport floor.

After three weeks of travel, I was ready to be home. So ready. My heart
and body were literally aching for my family, for my own bed, for the
rhythms of my "normal" life. The storm system that settled over the city
of Chicago was unmoved by my ache. My flight home got cancelled.
I was stuck in a crowded airport, forced to spend another night away
from the comforts of home.

Exhausted and at the end of my rope, I sat down on the floor in the
middle of the airport terminal and bawled. My fellow travelers rushed by
with their rolling suitcases and gawked. I've never felt more alone.

In my distress, I reached out to a friend who has prayed me through
many crises, big and small.

"I'm stuck in the airport and can't get home," I sobbed, as soon as Dree
answered her phone.

Immediately, she started praying out loud. As she asked the Lord to
comfort me, the tears stopped streaming down my face. The Holy Spirit
had been with me all along, but Dree's prayers helped me be aware of His
presence when all I saw were strangers and cold airport benches. I was
going to be okay, I realized. My friend's prayers gave me the strength I
needed to stand up and carry on.

Dree couldn't do anything about my cancelled flight. She couldn't get me
home that night. But by praying she reminded me that Jesus was with

me in the airport terminal. When distress stole my peace, she carried my burdens to Him through prayer.

Scripture is clear that the children of God are to pray for each other. We find the command in James 5:16 as the second half of God's instruction to confess our sin to one another: "Therefore, confess your sins to one another and pray for one another, that you may be healed. The prayer of a righteous person has great power as it is working."

We owe it to each other to go to war against sin along with the emotions that come with living in a world as broken as ours—discouragement, defeat, despair. How do we do it? We pray for one another. Confession and prayer are the gifts we keep handing each other and the most powerful weapons we have at our disposal.

Prayer matters because it gets to the heart of God (2 Chron. 7:14), but prayer also matters because of the ways it changes *our* hearts. Try to remain indifferent about someone you're committed to pray for. You can't. Prayer is an invisible chord that ties our hearts together.

Prayer is the love language of God's people. Close your eyes. Consider the "one anothers" all around you; the faces around your breakfast table, the fellow parents in the carpool line, the crying woman sitting on the airport floor . . . Practically, how do you live out God's command to love one another? It's easier than you think. Pray and keep praying.

CONSIDER:

Recall a time when someone else prayed for you and it made a significant difference in your life. Have you taken the time to thank them? Why not do so today?

_____

_____

_____

PRAY:

Make a list of the "one anothers" you interact with daily. Start with your family. Expand to your friends. Consider the strangers and acquaintances you rub shoulders with every day: the person who delivers your mail, the secretary at your child's school, the neighbor you wave at on your walk each morning . . . Don't let this command stay theoretical. Pray for the "one anothers" the Lord brings to mind right now.

TRUST:

Is someone regularly praying for you? If not, do you feel comfortable asking for prayer? This week, ask someone to pray for you, trusting that when you do you are helping them live and love like Christ calls them to.

> I appeal to you, brothers, by our Lord Jesus Christ and by the love of the Spirit, to strive together with me in your prayers to God on my behalf. (Romans 15:30)

DO:

Often the first thing we offer one another is our input. Commit to pray for others as a first response, holding your thoughts and opinions until you have prayed for (and as often as possible, prayed with) those who have expressed their needs to you.

DAY 20

Therefore encourage one another
and build one another up,
just as you are doing.

1 THESSALONIANS 5:11

BUILD *One Another* UP

My life is built on the firm foundation of God's Word. But if we could see with our physical eyes the realities of what happens in the spiritual realm, I have no doubt I would see the words of others as the scaffold that holds me up and helps me to stand firm.

The time a coworker called me "a deep well" comes to mind, along with the moment my pastor announced that I really know my Bible and the countless times my husband has told me I am loved, cherished, and important. Words matter, especially when those words confirm the identity we have in Christ.

No wonder God calls each of us to the ministry of encouragement.

"Therefore encourage one another and build one another up, just as you are doing" (1 Thess. 5:11).

A little Bible scholar trick is to intentionally pause to ask what the "therefore" is there for when we find that little word in Scripture. In this case, the "therefore" points us to the big reason why we should take the time to speak life-giving words to each other. It's not because we should traffic in warm fuzzies. The reason is bigger, *much* bigger . . .

> For you yourselves are fully aware that the day of the Lord will come like a thief in the night. While people are saying, "There is peace and security," then sudden destruction will come upon them as labor pains come upon a pregnant woman, and they will not escape. But you are not in darkness, brothers, for that day to surprise you like a thief.

For you are all children of light, children of the day. We are not of the night or of the darkness. So then let us not sleep, as others do, but let us keep awake and be sober. For those who sleep, sleep at night, and those who get drunk, are drunk at night. But since we belong to the day, let us be sober, having put on the breastplate of faith and love, and for a helmet the hope of salvation. For God has not destined us for wrath, but to obtain salvation through our Lord Jesus Christ. (vv. 2–9)

The eight verses that precede the command to build others up aren't about happy words and Hallmark card sentiments; they're about the return of Christ. Through this lens, we see six reasons to intentionally build up our brothers and sisters in Christ.

1. The day of the Lord is coming.
2. This should not surprise us.
3. We are children of the light and of the day, *not* children of the darkness or of the night.
4. Since we know Jesus is coming, we need to watch for Him.
5. As we watch, we need to protect our hearts with faith and love and our minds with the hope of our salvation.
6. Because of Jesus, our destiny is hope, not wrath.

When you send the note of encouragement you've been meaning to write, when you take the time to text a friend that you see Christ working in her heart, when you pause to say thank you to someone for building up the kingdom, you are choosing not to waste the wait by pointing others to the promised hope of Christ's imminent return.

When the "one anothers" around us are wilting under the weight of brokenness, when the cares of life bend our shoulders or clench our fists, when hope feels far off . . . we have a plan for that.

"Encourage one another and build one another up, just as you are doing."

CONSIDER:

Consider a time when the encouraging words of another Christ-follower made a difference in your life. What was it about their words that made such an impact?

_____

_____

_____

PRAY:

Ask the Lord to help you see who has lost hope around you and to know how to build them up.

TRUST:

Jesus is coming back. He really is! That is a source of permanent hope for every Christ-follower, so let's remind each other of His return often.

> "Behold, I am coming soon, bringing my recompense with me, to repay each one for what he has done. I am the Alpha and the Omega, the first and the last, the beginning and the end." (Revelation 22:12–13)

DO:

Put today's verse into action by intentionally building someone else up with words that point them to our hope in Christ.

DAY 21

Let the word of Christ dwell
in you richly, teaching and
admonishing one another in all
wisdom, singing psalms and
hymns and spiritual songs,
with thankfulness in your
hearts to God.

COLOSSIANS 3:16

TEACHING AND ADMONISHING
One Another

What is your role in the Body of Christ?

Perhaps you're on the welcome team, handing out bulletins and directing people to the bathrooms. Or you do the vacuuming or deliver meals. Maybe you play the piano. Are you the one that people trust to listen to their pains and pray for them?

I have news for you: no matter what you're doing or your gifting, you're a teacher!

Teaching is not just a job for the pastor or Sunday school teachers. It's part of the everyday life of the Body of Christ. Just rubbing shoulders with other believers and living alongside them is a way of teaching.

Think about it. Who have you learned the most from? Your pastor or some other Bible teacher may immediately come to mind. Or, if you think more broadly, maybe it's your grandmother who taught you family recipes and your spiritual heritage. Or a mentor who showed you how to do your job more effectively. Or a friend who practices a simple transformative habit that you now do, too.

Teaching is sometimes expounding Greek and Hebrew verbs from a pulpit. But it's also helping a young person have wisdom in dating and showing someone the love of God through a hand on their shoulder.

It's whatever ways we help our fellow believers embrace and understand the word of Christ—and obey it.

Think about it this way. There's more than one way to clean yourself. You can do it here and there, camping-style, using a cloth, washing parts of your body but never getting completely wet, or you can jump in the shower or tub and get all sudsy and rinsed.

Scripture talks about being cleansed by the washing of water with the word (Eph. 5:26). The preaching and teaching of the Word in a class or service is one way to "get wet" with the Word of God—and it's an essential one. But if the Word of God is to *dwell* in us—make itself at home in us—we need more than just a sponge bath on Sunday. We need to be soaked.

Personal time in the Word has a role in this, but so does spending time with other believers. Seeing how they walk with Jesus, live with their families, and love their neighbors, plus hearing their words spoken into our lives, are important ways that we can be completely drenched in the Word of God.

Our verse tells us that teaching each other, admonishing (correcting) each other, singing songs that worship God, and giving thanks are all ways that we can give ourselves a good Word of God shower.

Not only can you learn from other believers, *you* also have a role in teaching. As you follow Jesus, learn from His Word, and are led and transformed by His Spirit—simply just living by faith—your life is teaching others.

CONSIDER:

Who are you learning from, and who is learning from you? Who could you be spending time with more intentionally?

_____

_____

_____

PRAY:

Thank God for the teachers in your life, past and present, and pray for the people who are teaching you today. Then ask Him to make you an effective teacher of the Word by your way of life.

TRUST:

As you teach others by your life and words, Jesus is with you. He will not forsake you.

> "Go therefore and make disciples of all nations, baptizing them in the name of the Father and of the Son and of the Holy Spirit, teaching them to observe all that I have commanded you. And behold, I am with you always, to the end of the age." (Matthew 28:19–20)

DO:

Look at your calendar for this week and next. Consider: Who are you going to be spending time with? Or are there opportunities to schedule some time to be with others? Is there something you can learn from them? What are you learning that you can teach them? Then use those ideas to help you intentionally teach by your life.

DAY 22

But exhort one another every day, as long as it is called "today," that none of you may be hardened by the deceitfulness of sin.

HEBREWS 3:13

EXHORT *One Another*

. . . .

Every time I see Kathy, she is talking about the Lord.

Kathy and I attend church together. We often greet each other in the
lobby on Sunday mornings and sit beside each other in ladies' Bible
studies. Occasionally, I bump into her in the grocery store, as my rowdy
children climb in and out of the cart. No matter the setting, regardless of
the challenges her day may have held, Kathy always has a kind word to
share. Most often it's a Bible verse she's memorized or a specific way she's
been praying. Instead of keeping these things to herself, she turns them
into exhortations, reminders of our identity in Christ. Her words have
made a difference in my life too many times to count.

Kathy doesn't approach exhortation as an activity. It's not simply another
box to check on her to-do list. For Kathy, pointing others to Jesus is
a *lifestyle*, something she has allowed the Lord to teach her to do all
day, every day. She isn't super-spiritual. She doesn't have a spiritual
superpower that you and I do not. She simply chooses to exhort the
"one anothers" all around her every chance she gets.

Listen to how the writer of Hebrews asks us to speak to one another:
"But exhort one another every day, as long as it is called 'today,' that none
of you may be hardened by the deceitfulness of sin." (Heb. 3:13)

When should we prioritize speaking words that exhort and encourage?
Only on days that end with a "y." Kathy lives this schedule.

On Mondays she exhorts.

On Tuesdays she exhorts.

Wednesdays? Yep, she exhorts.

Thursday, Friday, Saturday, and Sunday. Exhort. Exhort. Exhort. Exhort.

Exhortation isn't a Sunday morning activity. It's an all day, every day decision to speak life-giving words that point the "one anothers" to Jesus. It's a little choice that makes a big difference, because we all need it, every single day.

Since we're living in a "today" right this very moment, we don't have to wait to apply this principle. Look into the eyes of your family, your coworkers, the guy at the gas station, the woman cutting your hair, and choose to live like Kathy. Speak a word of exhortation today.

CONSIDER:

Do you have a "Kathy" in your world? Someone who takes the time to point you to the Lord often? What difference have their words made in your life?

_____

_____

_____

PRAY:

Ask the Lord to show you how to exhort others well. Listen and respond as the Holy Spirit nudges you to speak words of encouragement or exhortation to others.

TRUST:

Your words matter.

> Let no corrupting talk come out of your mouths, but only such as is good for building up, as fits the occasion, that it may give grace to those who hear. (Ephesians 4:29)

DO:

Set a goal to share a word of exhortation/encouragement every day for the next seven days. Pay attention to how this activity impacts your own heart as well as the attitudes of those you choose to exhort.

DAY 23

Encourage one another with
these words.

1 THESSALONIANS 4:18

ENCOURAGE *One Another*

My favorite Greek word is *parakaleo*.

Yes, I'm a word nerd. Indulge me for a moment.

This is a word that gets translated so many different ways that it's the basis of *three* different devotional days in this book! (It's translated *encourage* in today's verse.) There's so many shades of meaning and depth here that it's hard to get it across in one English word. So, for someone who loves words, it's a good one.

You may not be someone who reads dictionaries for fun. It's an unusual hobby, I'll admit. So, rather than a synonym list, here are some mental pictures to give you an idea of this word's meaning:

- A coach's pep talk at halftime of a brutal game.
- A sympathy card sent to a friend after the loss of a loved one.
- An invitation to a joyful event.
- A tutor teaching a difficult concept to a student.
- A parent's instruction to a toddler or advice to a young adult child.
- An intervention staged by an addict's loved ones.
- A gentle word spoken in a difficult moment.
- A fan cheering on a marathon runner.
- A counselor calming a panicked client.
- A warning sign in a dangerous area.
- A summons from a king.
- A friend's words pushing you in the right direction.

Parakaleo is an onion type of word. You peel back a layer of definition, and there's another, and another. So, when we're called to encourage, comfort, or admonish in Scripture, all of these different meanings encompass it. It's using our words to love our brothers and sisters, and there are so many ways to do that.

There are a few other reasons I love this word: it's a spiritual gift (that I've been told that I have), it's fun to say, and, most importantly, it's what the Holy Spirit does for us.

> "I will ask the Father, and he will give you another Helper, to be with you forever, even the Spirit of truth. . . . the Helper, the Holy Spirit, whom the Father will send in my name, he will teach you all things and bring to your remembrance all that I have said to you. Peace I leave with you; my peace I give to you. Not as the world gives do I give to you. Let not your hearts be troubled, neither let them be afraid." (John 14:16–17, 26–27)

When we cheer on other believers in using their gifts, speak a word of comfort to a grieving friend, call a friend back from sin to the Lord, or teach our children something new about God, we're practicing encouragement. We're doing the work of *parakaleo*. We're walking in the way of the Spirit.

Whether you need to warn or encourage or counsel or exhort or comfort someone today, ask the Lord to help you do it in the Spirit of power *and* love *and* self-control (2 Tim. 1:7). Because even if you can peel back all the layers of definition, love is at the heart of the onion of *parakaleo*. Without it, all our attempts at using our words will rot and fall apart.

CONSIDER:

How are you uniquely gifted or placed to speak into another believer's life? Is there someone who could use encouragement from you?

_____

_____

_____

PRAY:

Use the words of this old hymn to guide your prayers today:

> Breathe on me, Breath of God,
> fill me with life anew,
> that I may love the way you love,
> and do what you would do.[3]

TRUST:

If you're a believer in Christ, the Holy Spirit dwells within you. He will help you to speak words of help, encouragement, and hope.

> "I [Jesus] will ask the Father, and he will give you another Helper, to be with you forever, even the Spirit of truth, whom the world cannot receive, because it neither sees him nor knows him. You know him, for he dwells with you and will be in you." (John 14:16–17)

DO:

Whether it's a pep talk, a comforting verse, or an invitation to do the right thing, speak or write a word of encouragement to someone today.

PART IV:
Your Actions

Having loved his own who were in the world, he loved them to the end. . . . He laid aside his outer garments, and taking a towel, tied it around his waist. Then he . . . began to wash the disciples' feet.

JOHN 13:1, 4–5

God shows his love for us in that while we were still sinners, Christ died for us.

ROMANS 5:8

DAY 24

Greet one another
with a holy kiss.

ROMANS 16:16

GREET *One Another*

. . . .

Hugs. Fist bumps. Kisses on the cheek. A good, firm handshake. Secret handshakes. A pat on the arm. A hand on the shoulder. A smile and a wave.

These are all ways that we greet each other. They welcome someone into our lives and provide a sense of recognition. We all know the warm rush of emotion when someone notices us, when they say, "Hey, you're one of my people!"

It's easy to greet the people we know well. Close friends, family members, business associates. But what about the people who are in the Church but we don't know as well? Or those who don't fit into our mold of what a Christian should be like? Or the people we just don't understand? Are they excluded from this command to greet believers?

We followers of Jesus are often prone to creating cliques, to greet those who greet us, to love those who love us, to give honor to those who seem more likely to bring us honor. All throughout the New Testament, we're warned about this. (See Luke 6:32–36; James 2:1–9.)

On some level, we're always going to be closer to some folks than others. That's just a fact of our finite being. We *can't* know everyone the same way. But that doesn't mean that those outside our inner circle are to be less loved or welcomed.

By greeting other believers, whether we know them well or not, we are acknowledging that we're part of one family—the family of God.

Perhaps you read today's verse and got uncomfortable. Maybe a kiss isn't in your "greeting vocabulary," or perhaps the person you're greeting would feel uncomfortable if you kissed them on the cheek! That's okay. The important thing here isn't the mode; it's the intention. It's the welcoming, giving the other person a sense of belonging, that matters.

So, here's your challenge: Greet your fellow brothers and sisters as "one anothers," as fellow heirs of eternal life. Greet them with holiness, with no hint of immorality or selfishness. Greet them with love (1 Peter 5:14). Greet them as if they're a member of your family—with holy kisses or fist bumps or handshakes or hugs—because they are.

CONSIDER:

Is there anyone in your church or Christian circle that you avoid greeting? Who do you have a hard time viewing as a member of the family of God?

_____

_____

_____

PRAY:

Ask God for grace in those difficult relationships—the folks you give a wide berth to, the eyes you try not to meet. Then seek Him for ways to receive them out of love rather than frustration or fear.

TRUST:

This is a hard word, but those who reject believers are walking the path to judgment. Whether your greetings are received well or not, God sees, and He honors your obedience.

> "As you enter the house, greet it. . . . And if anyone will not receive you or listen to your words, shake off the dust from your feet when you leave that house or town. Truly, I say to you, it will be more bearable on the day of judgment for the land of Sodom and Gomorrah than for that town." (Matthew 10:12, 14-15)

DO:

When you walk into church, say hello to the people you encounter, whether you know them or not. As appropriate, give them a hug, holy kiss, or handshake. Look them in the eye, and let them know that they're welcome into your life and in the family of God.

DAY 25

Show hospitality to one another
without grumbling.

1 PETER 4:9

SHOW HOSPITALITY TO
One Another

"Let's get together sometime."

"Bless her heart."

"Those shoes are so . . . interesting."

One of the complaints I've heard about American culture is that we tend to say phrases like this to cover up what we're really feeling.

We can give an outward appearance of welcome and kindness while inwardly feeling the opposite.

"Let's end this conversation so I can get on to the next thing."

"She is *really* dumb, but look at how nice I am not to say it!"

"Wow, those shoes are hideous!"

If we were honest with ourselves, that's likely what we really mean. And if we were *really* honest . . . we'd realize that, in many cases, this isn't just a cultural issue. It's a heart issue. It's a sinful human nature issue.

The Christians in Peter's day must have had a similar issue for him to give the instruction in today's verse. He says, "Show hospitality to one another [fellow Christians] *without grumbling*."

It's not just "welcome strangers" with a fake grin of "glad to see you." It's a heart-welcome that is sincere and doesn't complain behind closed doors.

It's also not just welcoming people you know. The Greek word for hospitality literally means "love of strangers." It's seeing a fellow believer not as a stranger but as a welcome friend. It's saying "come on in," and seeing to their needs. Why? Because hospitality looks like God.

He delivers us out of slavery to sin. He keeps us from figuratively sleeping on the streets. He welcomes us in as part of His family.

> Remember that you were at that time separated from Christ, alienated from the commonwealth of Israel and *strangers to the covenants of promise*, having no hope and without God in the world. But now in Christ Jesus you who once were far off have been brought near by the blood of Christ. . . . So then *you are no longer strangers* and aliens, but you are fellow citizens with the saints and members of the household of God. (Eph. 2:12–13, 19)

You were a stranger, and God showed you wholehearted hospitality. He didn't say "welcome" and mean the opposite, and He isn't complaining about your presence in His family. On the contrary! When you were His enemy, Christ died for you. What pure-hearted hospitality!

So, what is the response of a stranger that's been welcomed in, blood-bought, and made a son or daughter? Generous hospitality to others, as if you were serving King Jesus Himself.

> "Then the King will say to those on his right, 'Come, you who are blessed by my Father, inherit the kingdom prepared for you from the foundation of the world. For I was hungry and you gave me food, I was thirsty and you gave me drink, I was a stranger and you welcomed me . . . Then the righteous will answer him, saying, 'Lord, when did we see you hungry and feed you, or thirsty and give you drink? And when did we see you a stranger and welcome you? . . . And the King will answer them, 'Truly, I say to you, as you did it to one of the least of these my brothers, *you did it to me.*'" (Matt. 25:34–35, 37–38, 40)

Open wide your doors, set another place at the table, and prepare your heart to love a stranger. After all, it's what your Father did for you.

CONSIDER:

Are your words and hospitality genuine? How could you practically welcome others to your table or in your life?

_____

_____

_____

PRAY:

Ask God to give you opportunities to love through hospitality and to guard you from grumbling when you do it.

TRUST:

God honors and rewards generous hospitality. He will provide all that you need to give and take care of your needs.

> "Give, and it will be given to you. Good measure, pressed down, shaken together, running over, will be put into your lap. For with the measure you use it will be measured back to you." (Luke 6:38)

DO:

Set an extra place at the table, invite a friend to coffee, or chat with a new coworker. Take a step of practicing hospitality today.

DAY 26

Love one another with brotherly
affection. Outdo one another
in showing honor.

ROMANS 12:10

OUTDO *One Another*
IN SHOWING HONOR

Imagine we're all in a race, every man, woman, and child. The way to advance is to show the most honor to our fellow racers. Pushing and shoving our way to the front of the pack is actually how we lose instead of win. This kind of race requires a relay format. I pass the baton to you by elevating you above myself, you pass the baton back to me by doing the same. The clear winner isn't the individual racers but the kingdom of Christ, which is celebrated when Christ's followers harmoniously celebrate each other.

No one has to teach our flesh the basics of one-upmanship. In our sinful, human state we naturally know how to vie for power, put others down, and look out for number one. Yet following Christ means learning to stop walking in the flesh and to walk in the spirit instead (Gal. 5:16). This often means radical changes in our interactions with one another. Instead of outdoing each other in the areas of success, power, wealth, and authority, the Bible invites us into a different kind of competition.

"Outdo one another in showing honor" (Rom. 12:10).

This is the upside down, inside out way that Christ introduced when He said, "So the last will be first, and the first last. . . . You know that the rulers of the Gentiles lord it over them, and their great ones exercise authority over them. It shall not be so among you. But whoever would be great among you must be your servant, and whoever would be first among you must be your slave, even as the Son of Man came not to be served but to serve, and to give his life as a ransom for many" (Matt. 20:16, 25–28).

"Winners" in the kingdom get to the place of victory by celebrating the "one anothers" all around them. If we try to outdo one another in showing off instead, everyone loses.

We'll never outdo one another in showing honor if our eyes are fixed on ourselves or even on the other racers. We must look to our forerunner, Jesus, who humbly honored others with His service and sacrifice even as the King of Kings.

CONSIDER:

What does it mean to "honor" others? List three practical ways you can show honor.

_____

_____

_____

PRAY:

Ask the Lord to help you embrace His call to others-first living and to teach you how to surrender your fleshly desire to elevate yourself.

TRUST:

If you prioritize true humility, Christ will lift you up.

> Humble yourselves before the Lord, and he will exalt you. (James 4:10)

DO:

Study Jesus' words recorded in Matthew 20:16–28. Consider anew the radical way He asks you to live.

DAY 27

"If I then, your Lord and Teacher,
have washed your feet,
you also ought to wash one
another's feet."

JOHN 13:14

WASH *One Another's* FEET

It was a week of church camp to go down in history.

What sticks out in my memory is not a Bible message or the food or any of the activities but the nurse. We basically became best friends that week.

My first day at the camp, while just walking—walking!—I tripped and fell and sprained my ankle badly and nearly passed out from the pain. (Definitely not my best moment.) Some of the counselors helped me over to a deck and then to the nurses' station. For sure, it was a hard thing to have my ankle wrapped and to not be able to play games, but that wasn't the worst of it.

That evening, I had my first ever asthma attack. Wheezing, coughing, gasping for breath. It was terrifying. The same nurse that wrapped my ankle was up late with me each night of that week, as wave after wave of breathing scares came.

I don't remember her name or even her face, but I remember her presence and her care. Though those evenings could be remembered as a nightmare, and though at times the ankle incident comes back to haunt me as a family joke ("Yeah, we all know you have issues with walking . . ."), my memories from that week are the opposite of terrible.

They're ones of a woman who was willing to serve the hot mess in front of her. They're ones of service through touch.

Hands wrapping my ankle.
Hands supporting me through a coughing fit.
Hands holding me up and helping me walk.

I remember this, and I pray, "Take *my* hands, and let them move / At the impulse of Thy love."

That's exactly what Jesus' command to "wash one another's feet" means. It's letting God's love and care for you move outward into love and care for others.

It's humbly doing the jobs no one else wants to, but it's also simply embodying His love.

It's holding a small child's hand. It's helping clean up a sick person's mess. It's providing a shoulder to cry on. It's seen in teenage boys playfully wrestling on the floor and a mother tenderly breastfeeding her newborn. Protective hugs, back rubs, a hand to help someone up, and yes, even washing someone's feet as an act of love—they can all be physical representations of the love Christ Himself has for us.

As God in the flesh, He touched. He washed. He put His hands on the sick.

"I have given you an example, that you also should do just as I have done to you" (John 13:15).

Today, do what's in front of you with your hands. Wipe away tears or messy residue, hand someone a tissue, or help the klutzy girl to the nurse's office.

When our hands move in love, we get to be His hands in a world that desperately needs His touch. So, let's "wash feet," however He directs. And maybe we'll create memories of His love for others.

CONSIDER:

What are your hands available to do in love? What are the needs right in front of you every day? How can you be the "hands of Jesus" today?

_____

_____

_____

PRAY:

Remember a time that someone ministered to you through touch. Speak that memory back to God, and thank Him for that person.

TRUST:

As you do good with your hands out of fear of the Lord and love for others, He will care for you and guide you in the way of His goodness.

> Blessed is everyone who fears the LORD,
> who walks in his ways!
> You shall eat the fruit of the labor of your hands;
> you shall be blessed, and it shall be well with you. (Psalm 128:1–2)

DO:

Keep an eye out for good work that your hands can do today—especially ways to minister to others through appropriate, kind touch.

DAY 28

So then, my brothers, when you
come together to eat,
wait for one another.

1 CORINTHIANS 11:33

WAIT FOR *One Another*

Recently, the elders at my church started doing something different when they served communion. Typically everyone in the congregation goes forward to receive the bread and wine. We shake hands or hug and speak the words "Peace be with you" to one another (or "pass the peace" as it's called in some faith traditions), and then the lines form.

"The body of Christ, which is for you."

"The blood of Christ, which is for you."

The words are repeated over and over again, as each person goes up to partake. This hasn't changed.

What has changed is that there are a few folks who no longer go forward. The elements are brought to them. In one of the front pews, an elderly couple sits, and they are served first, before the line. He has dementia, and she sits with stately, feminine valor by his side. He can no longer go forward to receive communion without difficulty.

All the energetic teenagers in the row behind . . . they have to wait an extra moment. The words are the same, the elements are the same, but the process takes just a little longer. This small moment each week is teaching all of us patience—and honor for these faithful saints.

In that extra minute or two, we are learning in a new way to wait for each other.

This is what Paul is talking about in today's verse. He's encouraging us to wait, to be patient with each other with expectation of what God is doing in their lives—and ours. We are "looking forward to the city . . . whose designer and builder is God," as Hebrews 11:10 puts it. By taking the time to wait for one another, we are infusing that faith with one-another love in the here-and-now.

In waiting, results may come slower, words may need to be repeated, hurry and timelines may need to be set aside. We may have to take a few extra minutes (or hours) to make sure someone feels heard in their pain. We may be made late for an appointment so our children can find their shoes (again!). We may have to spend extra time teaching a coworker to do a task instead of just doing it ourselves.

All of these moments of learning to wait for each other, no matter how small . . . they're God's means of forming patience in us. This kind of momentary patience reflects our sure hope in the tomorrow—when waiting will end, dementia will no longer exist, children's possessions will not be hopelessly lost, patience will not be needed, and we will be completely unhurried in the eternal presence of our God.

So, today, don't rush past the waiting. Embrace it.

CONSIDER:

Who are the people that you find hardest to wait for? How do you respond to them?

_____

_____

_____

PRAY:

Confess any impatience that the Holy Spirit has convicted you of, and ask the Lord to help you wait with patience for the people you encounter today.

TRUST:

Your Lord is coming. A harvest is promised. The waiting will end.

> Be patient, therefore, brothers, until the coming of the Lord. See how the farmer waits for the precious fruit of the earth, being patient about it, until it receives the early and the late rains. You also, be patient. Establish your hearts, for the coming of the Lord is at hand. (James 5:7–8)

DO:

Make an intentional choice to wait for another person today. Step into a longer line, give your toddler your full attention, or stay on hold when you'd like to hang up. While you do it, thank God for an opportunity to practice His loving patience.

DAY 29

Do not deprive one another,
except perhaps by agreement
for a limited time, that you may
devote yourselves to prayer; but
then come together again,
so that Satan may not tempt you
because of your lack
of self-control.

1 CORINTHIANS 7:5

DO NOT DEPRIVE
One Another

Someone in Corinth was brave enough to write the apostle Paul an awkward letter. We know that because 1 Corinthians 7 opens with "Now concerning the matters about which you wrote . . ." Paul answers with instructions for sexual intimacy between husbands and wives.

I'm so grateful a fellow Christian was brave enough to ask hard questions about the practicalities of loving "one another," and I'm so grateful that God's Word preserves Paul's wise, helpful answer. As I seek to move the "one another" principles from theory to action, I need every nudge, encouragement, and reminder Scripture has to give.

The challenges of treating "one another" like Christ calls us to don't stay in public spheres. They follow us to our kitchen table, into our most vulnerable conversations, and behind closed bedroom doors.

At all times, in every arena, God calls us to surrender our selfishness and to prioritize the needs of others above our own. There isn't a space in our lives where we get a pass on loving "one another." In the context of marriage, that means we don't use the gift of sex to gain power over each other, to manipulate, or to control. Instead, we remember God's command to "love one another" and refuse to allow the gift of sexual intimacy to ever become a weapon.

The Word of God is not a buffet. We don't get to pick and choose what applies and what doesn't because, "All Scripture is breathed out by God and profitable for teaching, for reproof, for correction, and for training in righteousness, that the man of God may be complete, equipped for every good work" (2 Tim. 3:16–17).

That means we can't take a buffet approach to the "one anothers" either. We don't selectively choose who we love, honor, and encourage. Instead, we ask the Holy Spirit to empower us to love the "one anothers" in public and behind closed doors.

What is it about the "one anothers" that feels awkward to you?

- Perhaps it's the clear call to clothe yourself in humility when your heart more naturally bends toward pride.

- Maybe it's the command to bear with one another when you're tempted to throw in the towel.

- Maybe the idea of confessing your sins to one another makes your palms sweat or Paul's admonition not to withhold intimacy from one another makes you feel out of control.

Don't respond to the awkward by dismissing the command. Open your Bible, again and again, and be encouraged—the "one anothers" are a gift, breathed from God, and useful for every area of your life.

CONSIDER:

Is your sex life something you've submitted to the authority of Scripture?

_____

_____

_____

PRAY:

Ask the Lord to reveal any area where you've decided loving the "one anothers" is optional.

TRUST:

Through God's Word and the power of His Spirit, you have everything you need to love the "one anothers" as Christ has called you to.

> His divine power has granted to us all things that pertain to life and godliness, through the knowledge of him who called us to his own glory and excellence. (2 Peter 1:3)

DO:

If you are married, do what Paul calls us to in today's verse by refusing to withhold the gift of sexual intimacy from your spouse unless you've discussed the matter with your spouse and both of you have agreed. Even then, limit this kind of restriction in your marriage.

If you are unmarried, honor the command found in Hebrews 13:4: "Let marriage be held in honor among all, and let the marriage bed be undefiled, for God will judge the sexually immoral and adulterous."

DAY 30

As each has received a gift, use
it to serve one another, as good
stewards of God's varied grace.

1 PETER 4:10

USE YOUR GIFTS TO SERVE
One Another

It's been my experience that when it comes to spiritual gifts, most of us fall into one of two categories. Either we don't know what our gifts are, or we are waiting for someone to give us permission to use them. There is a third category I've observed less frequently. These are Christians who know what their gifts are and know how to use them, but they've convinced themselves that because of burnout, or because they were not celebrated as they'd hoped to be, that it's okay to warm the bench and put their God-given gifts back in the box.

I've made it one of my missions in life to move others into a fourth category. Individuals in this category know their gifts, see their on-ramps to use them for the good of the Church, and get busy having an impact on God's kingdom. This is the category I want to live in every day of my life. It's the category I want you to live every day of your life in, too. I have a hard time settling for anything less. Because your gifts belong to me. And my gifts? Well, they belong to you.

Paul teaches us this concept with a powerful word picture found in 1 Corinthians 12:

> Now concerning spiritual gifts, brothers, I do not want you to be uninformed. . . . For just as the body is one and has many members, and all the members of the body, though many, are one body, so it is with Christ. . . . The eye cannot say to the hand, "I have no need of you," nor again the head to the feet, "I have no need of you." . . . But God has so composed the body, giving greater honor to the part that lacked it, that there may be no division in the body, but that

the members may have the same care for one another. If one member suffers, all suffer together; if one member is honored, all rejoice together. Now you are the body of Christ and individually members of it. (vv. 12:1, 12, 21, 24–27)

There is no spleen in the kingdom of God. When you use your gifts, it benefits me. When I use my gifts, it benefits you. And when we don't, the whole body suffers.

I love the simple, straightforward command found in Romans 12:6: "Having gifts that differ according to the grace given to us, let us use them."

You've got God-given gifts. Get busy using them! It's one way you can choose to love the "one anothers." Do you have the gift of service? Use it to bless the "one anothers." Are you a gifted teacher? Teach the "one anothers"! Are you gifted in prayer? Pray for the "one anothers."

Our gifts aren't meant to sit on a shelf and be observed. They are meant to be given back and forth among the children of God. As we close the cover on this devotional, with a new awareness of the "one anothers" all around us, may we learn to live in the fourth category—daily using our gifts to serve others and build up the kingdom of Christ.

CONSIDER:

Do you know what your spiritual gifts are? Do you see them as belonging to the "one anothers" in your life?

_____

_____

_____

PRAY:

Ask the Lord to help you maximize your gifts for the good of His kingdom.

TRUST:

As you use your gifts to bless others, God is multiplying your efforts toward a greater, more significant gain.

> To each is given the manifestation of the Spirit for the common good. (1 Corinthians 12:7)

DO:

Close this final devotion by reflecting on all you've learned about the "one anothers" in Scripture these thirty days. Spend time in prayer, thanking God for His heart for His children and ask Him to teach you to live with a "one anothers" mindset that honors Him.

A Closing Blessing

(from Jude)

But you, beloved,
building yourselves up in your most holy faith and praying in the Holy Spirit,
keep yourselves in the love of God,
waiting for the mercy of our Lord Jesus Christ that leads to eternal life. . . .

Now to him who is able to keep you from stumbling
and to present you blameless before the presence of his glory
with great joy,
to the only God, our Savior,
through Jesus Christ our Lord, be glory, majesty, dominion, and authority,
before all time and now and forever.

Amen.

Meet Our Staff Contributors

Hayley Mullins is learning to love through living with a family of ten and practicing "the one anothers" at a small Presbyterian church in northern Indiana. She is currently the managing editor at *Revive Our Hearts*, where she gets to cultivate grammar, coach staff writers, and curate blog posts that point readers to Jesus.

Erin Davis is learning to encourage the "one anothers" at her breakfast table. She is the content manager for *Revive Our Hearts*, where she gets to invite women to drink from the deep well of God's Word through Bible-centered resources like this one. She is the author of several books and Bible studies including, *Connected: Curing the Pandemic of Everyone Feeling Alone Together, Beyond Bath Time,* and the My Name is Erin series.

Notes

J.H. Jowett, "Tending the Flock," *Epistles of St. Peter*, Third Edition (London: Hodder and Stoughton, 1910), http://www.ccel.org/ccel/jowett/epistpeter.iii. vii.html?scrBook=1Pet&scrCh=5-5&scrV=5-5#iii.xvii-p0.1.

William Ernest Henley, "Invictus," https://www.poetryfoundation.org/ poems/51642/invictus.

Edwin Hatch, "Breathe on Me, Breath of God," *Hymnary.org*, https:// hymnary.org/text/breathe_on_me_breath_of_god.

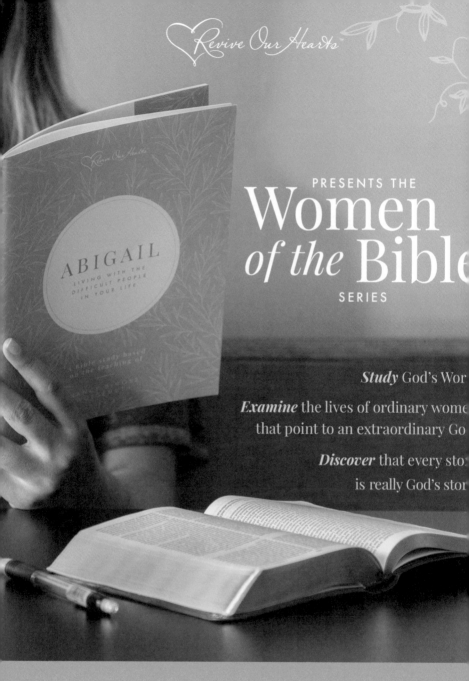

Revive Our Hearts™

PRESENTS THE

Women
of the Bible
SERIES

ABIGAIL
LIVING WITH THE
DIFFICULT PEOPLE
IN YOUR LIFE

Study God's Wor

Examine the lives of ordinary wome
that point to an extraordinary Go

Discover that every sto
is really God's stor

Join the conversation about these studies through the
Women of the Bible podcast. Listen in as women open God's
Word and walk through each study together.

REVIVEOURHEARTS.COM/WOMENOFTHEBIBLE

MORE FROM

Revive Our Hearts™

RADIO • EVENTS • BLOGS

LEADERS

REVIVE OUR **HEARTS** . COM